The Red-Crowned Crane

The Red-Crowned Crane

By Edward Voeller

DILLON PRESS, INC.
Minneapolis, Minnesota 55415

Photographic Acknowledgments

The photographs are reproduced through the courtesy of Edward Voeller and the International Crane Foundation.

Library of Congress Cataloging-in-Publication Data

Voeller, Edward A.
The Red-crowned crane / Edward Voeller.

(A Dillon remarkable animals book)
Includes index.
Summary: Discusses the appearance, behavior, habitat, and current status of the red-crowned crane.

ISBN 0-87518-417-0 : $12.95
1. Japanese crane—Juvenile literature. [1. Japanese crane]
I. Title. II. Series.
QL696.G84V64   1989
598'.31—dc 20   89-11718
                                                                        CIP
                                                                        AC

Dillon Press, Inc., 242 Portland Avenue South
Minneapolis, Minnesota 55415

Printed in the United States of America
1 2 3 4 5 6 7 8 9 10 98 97 96 95 94 93 92 91 90 89

Contents

Facts about the
Red-Crowned Crane

Scientific Name: *Grus japonensis*

Description:

Length—56 inches (140 centimeters)

Wing Span—96 inches (240 centimeters)

Weight—22 to 30 pounds (10 to 14 kilograms)

Physical Features—Three toes plus shorter toe on back of foot; long legs, neck, and bill; large wings; and scaly feet and legs

Color—White with black forehead, throat, and neck; black feathers on inner parts of wings; a patch of red skin on top of head which turns brighter when the crane becomes excited or angry

Distinctive Habits: Loud, trumpetlike call which can be heard for more than two miles (3.2 kilometers); special actions and movements known as the crane dance; sleeps with one leg pulled up under the body

Food: Small fish, tadpoles, frogs, snakes, salamanders, and small mammals, such as mice and moles; also, baby birds, snails, worms, insects, buds and roots of marsh plants, corn, and buckwheat

Reproductive Cycle: Pairs mate for life; in late April or early May, female lays two eggs, usually only one of which hatches in four weeks; both parents share duties of hatching and raising; baby crane remains with parents for ten months

Life Span: 30 years or more in the wild; one crane lived to be 61 in captivity

Range: Marshy wetlands of northeast Asia: Hokkaido in Japan, Siberia in the Soviet Union, northern China

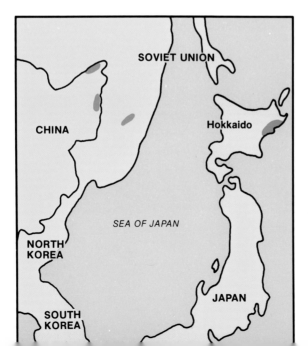

The red area on this map shows the range of the red-crowned crane.

タンチョウ *Grus japonensis*

20

自然保護

日本郵便 NIPPON

Red-crowned cranes on a Japanese postage stamp.

Chapter 1

A Treasured Animal

Almost half of the red-crowned cranes in the world make their home on the island of Hokkaido in northern Japan. Although the red-crowned crane is also known as the Japanese crane, this bird can be found in northern China and Siberia in the Soviet Union, too.

For as long as the red-crowned crane has lived in Japan, it has also lived in the hearts of the people there. Pictures of the crane appear on paper money and postage stamps, and the red-crowned crane is often used to decorate **kimonos*** because the bird is a symbol of long life and happiness. Also, Japanese of all ages enjoy making little **origami** cranes out of folded paper.

There are stories, songs, and poems about the

*Words in **bold type** are explained in the glossary at
the end of this book.

A red-crowned crane appears on this kimono.

red-crowned crane, too. One famous tale, "The Grateful Crane," is known to every Japanese boy and girl. In this story a poor woodcutter and his wife live alone in a cabin in the mountains of northern Japan. Their lives are changed when a mysterious visitor comes to their home.

The Grateful Crane

On his way home after a day in the forest, the old woodcutter heard a cry coming from the nearby marsh. Thinking someone was in trouble, the woodcutter followed the sound and found a beautiful white crane with large tears in its eyes, and its leg in a hunter's trap. The woodcutter quickly released the crane, and the bird flew away. This made the old man feel good.

At home that evening the woodcutter and his wife heard a soft knock at their cabin door. They opened the door and found a young girl shivering in the cold.

"I am lost, and I don't have a home," said the girl in tears. "Please let me stay with you."

The woodcutter and his wife welcomed the girl into their small cabin, and they fed her and gave her warm clothes. The lonely old couple was very happy to have a daughter.

That night when they were asleep, the girl got out of bed and began to work at the old woman's

11

loom. In the morning she gave the woodcutter and his wife the most beautiful piece of white cloth they had ever seen.

"Take this cloth to the market," she told them. "Sell it for a high price."

Soon the woodcutter and his wife had enough food in their cabin to last for months, because every night for more than a week the girl wove cloth for the couple to sell.

But the woodcutter was worried.

"You must sleep at night," he told the girl, "or you will be ill."

"I have much work to do," replied the girl.

Late that night the woodcutter woke up and went to the loom. There he found a beautiful crane weaving cloth from its white feathers. Then, right before the woodcutter's eyes, the crane changed into the girl.

"Now you know who I am," said the girl. "I came here to repay your kindness to me, but now I must leave."

Like "The Grateful Crane," this crane flies off in the darkness.

The girl said good-bye to the old couple, and then ran out of the cabin. Outside, she changed into a crane. Spreading its wings, the crane took off into the starry night. The bird looked down upon the old woodcutter and his wife as it circled above them. Then it disappeared.

Beauty and Grace

The respect shown for the red-crowned crane in this Japanese folktale is not surprising to those who have seen these beautiful birds in the fields and marshes of Hokkaido.

In winter, the red-crowned crane slowly stretches its long neck and picks tiny pieces of corn off a snow-covered field. In summer, the crane takes high and light steps as it wades for fish in the marshes of northern Japan. This tall, white bird seems to do everything with long, graceful movements.

The red-crowned crane is even more graceful in flight. It takes off from the ground, never from a tree. And because of its size and weight, it needs a good run to get started. First, it flaps its large wings to warm up, and then it runs into the wind like an airplane. Picking up speed, and with its long neck straight out, the red-crowned crane almost floats away from the ground. In the air, the bird's wings move slowly downward, quickly upward, and slowly down again. Soon the crane reaches

Two cranes run into the wind as they prepare to fly *(top)*. The crane flies with its neck straight out *(bottom)*.

great heights, and is the envy of anyone who has ever dreamed of flying.

An Unusual Animal

The red-crowned crane is admired for more than its great beauty and grace. People are also impressed by its unusual behavior and habits.

The great call of the red-crowned crane, for example, has fascinated people for ages. The crane appears to be calling all animals to attention with its loud trumpeting sound, which can be heard for a distance of more than two miles (3.2 kilometers). Sometimes the call is a cry of joy; at other times it is a warning.

The dance of the red-crowned crane is also unusual in the animal world. The crane bows, turns in a circle, arches its neck, and kicks up its feet in this short and interesting ceremony.

Some of the habits of the red-crowned crane are almost humanlike. These birds live in family units, for example, not in large flocks, and they are

In winter, a red-crowned crane kicks up its feet at the end of the crane dance.

A pair of cranes walks across a snow-covered field in Hokkaido.

faithful to their mates. Cranes pair up and stay together for life—only when a partner dies will a crane search for a new mate. Also, the work of raising a family is shared by crane couples.

Finally, the red-crowned crane lives too long to be considered just an ordinary animal. **Ornithologists**, scientists who study birds, estimate that cranes live to be 30 years or more in the wild. In a zoo one crane lived to be 61, and another is said to have died at 87! An old belief in Japan is untrue, however; red-crowned cranes do not live to be a thousand years old.

An Endangered Bird

To be able to watch a red-crowned crane or listen to its call in the wild is an exciting experience. Unfortunately, it is also a rare experience, because there are very few of these beautiful birds left today. Wildlife experts have placed the red-crowned crane on the **endangered species** list, which means that this bird could disappear if care is not taken to protect it and its marshy **habitat**. One way to help the red-crowned crane is to learn more about it. This will provide information about its habits, and how we can help it survive.

A red-crowned crane in flight.

Chapter 2

King of
the Marsh

The red-crowned crane belongs to a family of birds that is very old; in fact, the crane may be the oldest kind of bird. Some kinds of cranes probably lived 60 million years ago when dinosaurs still roamed the earth. Cranes have changed since then, but scientists know that the sandhill crane of North America looks much the same as it did 9 million years ago. In Japan, 4,000-year-old bones of the red-crowned crane have been found.

Today there are 15 kinds, or species, of **Gruidae**, the scientific name for the crane family. The red-crowned crane is one member of this family. Another is the whooping crane, which lives in Canada and the United States. The whooping crane is probably the closest relative of the red-crowned crane.

What is a Crane?

A crane is a tall bird with long legs, a long neck, and a long bill, but this also describes herons, egrets, storks, and flamingos, and none of these birds is related to the crane.

A closer look at these birds reveals important differences among them. A heron wading in a pond looks like a crane, but the heron is smaller. In flight a heron pulls its head back close to its body, and flies with its neck in an *S* shape. A crane flies with its neck and legs extended straight out.

Herons, storks, and egrets have four toes, so they can perch in trees. Cranes have only three full-length toes. Although cranes also have a very short fourth toe high on the heels of their feet, the toe is not long enough to let them grasp onto the branch of a tree. This is why cranes nest on the ground.

Storks are not as slim and tall as cranes, and they have thicker necks and bills. Stork babies, or chicks, must stay in the nest for several weeks

Cranes have three full-length toes and a short fourth toe.

after they hatch, but crane chicks leave the nest the day they are born. Also, storks are voiceless birds, while cranes have a loud call.

Flamingos are always pink, and they have webbed feet, like the feet of a duck. These brightly colored birds nest in large flocks; cranes, on the other hand, nest in pairs.

The Red-Crowned Crane

A red patch on the top of its head, or crown, gives this crane its name. The bird does not have any red feathers, though; the crane's crown is just a patch of bare, rough skin. When the red-crowned crane becomes excited or angry, the red crown gets brighter and larger.

The red-crowned crane is mostly white, but the throat, neck, and forehead are black on the adult bird. When it is standing, the crane looks like it has a black tail, but the long black feathers that droop over the tail are actually on the inner parts of the bird's wings.

The eyes of the red-crowned crane are dark brown. The bird has a greenish-brown bill, and its legs and feet are black and scaly, like the skin of a snake. The crane's long bill and sharp claws on its feet can be used as weapons.

While the male and female red-crowned crane look alike, the female is slightly smaller than the male. From the tip of its bill to the tip of its tail, the

The red-crowned crane has a red patch of skin on its head and long, black feathers that droop over its tail.

adult male is about 56 inches (140 centimeters) long, and it stands almost as tall as some human adults. The bird's **wingspan** is about 96 inches (240 centimeters), and it weighs about 26 pounds (12 kilograms).

Although red-crowned cranes are large birds, their hollow bones help make them light enough to fly. They are also very strong animals; if a red-crowned crane were as heavy as a human being, it would be seven times as strong. The crane needs strong muscles for flight.

Crane Communication

Four thousand years ago, people drew pictures of cranes on the wall of a cave. Like people today, they found the red-crowned crane an exciting animal to watch. The strange and interesting movements of the crane dance are especially fascinating.

The dance begins without warning. The bird suddenly starts to walk with stiff legs, and then it turns in a circle with its head high and bill pointed up. Quickly the red-crowned crane lowers its head almost to the ground. Now its neck is in the shape of a *U*, and its wings are raised a little. All at once the crane leaps into the air, kicks up its feet, and throws some grass or a twig into the air with a foot. Then the dance is over.

Only the red-crowned cranes know the reason for the dance, but ornithologists know the movements have some meaning. The crane dance is performed in all seasons, but it is especially frequent in February when some cranes are looking for mates. Also, crane couples sometimes perform the dance together. For these reasons, scientists think the dance may be intended to show that two birds are partners, or that a bird wants to claim a partner.

The call of the red-crowned crane is also used to communicate. When it makes its loud, trumpet-like call, the crane seems to be announcing something very important. This unforgettable sound comes from deep inside the crane. The call is difficult to describe, but it sounds in some ways like the

A crane couple dances together.

call of a pheasant. The call of the red-crowned crane, however, has high and low tones, and a certain rhythm or pattern.

Ko-kew, ko-kew, calls the male. Sometimes the female joins him in a duet: *ko-ko-kew, ko-ko-kew*, she answers. Other cranes sometimes pick up the call until six or seven birds are trumpeting together.

Special equipment allows the red-crowned crane to make this loud call. The crane's extra long windpipe, or **trachea**, is not straight. Some of it is coiled up in the breastbone, or **sternum**, in the bird's chest. The long, coiled trachea vibrates when the crane makes its call and, as a result, it works almost like a brass horn.

With its loud trumpetlike call, the red-crowned crane acts like the most important animal in the marshy wetlands. Long ago, the native **Ainu** people of Hokkaido in northern Japan thought so, too. They called the red-crowned crane the "king of the marsh."

In Hokkaido, a red-crowned crane wades in the shallow waters of a marsh.

Chapter 3

At Home in Hokkaido

A sign near the marsh on the island of Hokkaido tells people: "Please do not disturb the red-crowned crane." Far across the broad marsh, two white specks are moving among the tall grass and reeds. Binoculars are necessary to get a better look at the pair of red-crowned cranes. It is against the law to go closer.

The Marsh
The law keeps people away from the red-crowned crane, and so does the marsh. From far away the home of the red-crowned crane looks like a soft, thick, green and brown carpet, but it is impossible to walk on because it is really a soft and soggy sponge of plants that have piled up in the water

The waters of the marsh form small islands where crane couples build their nests.

over many years. Streams, canals, and small rivers wind their way through the marsh, forming little islands. Some of these islands have dry raised areas called **hummocks** where the crane couple makes a nest. The tall grass and reeds of the marsh help hide the nest from **predators**.

All members of the crane family make their

homes in marshy wetlands around the world, except in South America. But cranes will not nest in a marsh that is small; in fact, one crane couple needs a marsh area almost a mile long and a mile wide (three square kilometers) or more. Each pair also needs a place that is far from people, and an area that has a good dry nesting spot.

The marsh is where the red-crowned crane finds its favorite foods. Small fish, tadpoles, and frogs make the best meals, but these cranes also feed on snakes, salamanders, angleworms and insects, and small **mammals** such as mice and moles. Dragonflies are a favorite food of baby cranes.

All cranes are **omnivorous**, which means they will eat both plants and animals. The buds and roots of marsh plants make delicious meals for the red-crowned crane, and the bird will also eat corn and buckwheat, and even carrots and cabbage. Small bits of food are swallowed whole by the crane, while large fish are cut in half with quick chops of the bird's long bill.

A red-crowned crane holds a fish in its bill.

Winter Homes

Most species of cranes **migrate** to warm areas when marshes freeze because they cannot find enough food during the winter. The red-crowned cranes in Siberia and northern China fly to warmer parts of Asia. In autumn they gather in large fields where they take off in a flock and fly in a circle, going higher and higher. Then they form a *V* or a straight line and head south.

The red-crowned cranes in Japan, however, do not leave Hokkaido. They are the only cranes that stay in a cold and snowy climate during the winter. Although most of the red-crowned cranes in Hokkaido leave the frozen marshes in winter, they move only a short distance to nearby farm fields, where they come in family groups to eat corn and buckwheat in the fields.

Danger

Foxes, bears, and dogs do not have any trouble spotting the red-crowned crane; the tall, white bird cannot easily hide from predators. The red-crowned crane chick has better **camouflage** because it remains a light brown color until it is almost three months old. It is not easy to see in the reeds and grass of the marsh. The baby bird is **prey** for many animals, however, and it cannot defend itself. Large birds such as crows and hawks will attack

and carry away crane chicks, and sometimes destroy and eat crane eggs.

People, not animals, are the greatest danger to the red-crowned crane. Although the cranes in Japan are not hunted, and are protected by law, growing cities are coming closer to the habitat of the crane, sometimes **polluting** marshes or frightening off wildlife. Unfortunately, wetlands are being lost in many places around the world. In all of Asia, there may be fewer than a thousand red-crowned cranes, and if more wetlands are lost, the red-crowned crane could disappear. Six other endangered species of cranes around the world could also become **extinct**.

But the danger is not only to cranes. Many other animals depend on healthy wetlands. The number of cranes is a good indicator of the condition of the wetlands. When there are few or no cranes, the wetlands may be small or polluted, and when there are many cranes, the wetlands are probably healthy. For this reason, scientists and

In the reeds and grass of a marsh, a young red-crowned crane has better camouflage than its parents.

conservationists are interested in the size of crane populations around the world.

In Japan, a sad chapter in the history of the red-crowned crane began more than a hundred years ago when many marshes were drained so that farmers could use the land to grow rice. As a result, the red-crowned crane disappeared. No one saw these birds in Japan anymore, and everyone was sorry.

Then, in 1924, people were very happy to learn that 24 red-crowned cranes had been sighted in a marsh in eastern Hokkaido. That number did not increase for many years, though.

In 1952, during a very cold winter, many of Hokkaido's red-crowned cranes appeared on farm fields near the marsh. Newspapers reported that the birds were looking for food, and that winter some farmers began to scatter corn and buckwheat on their fields for the hungry cranes. Japanese schoolchildren were taken to see the rare white birds, and to make a count of the cranes.

A farmer scatters grain on a snow-covered field for hungry red-crowned cranes.

Since then, schoolchildren have counted the red-crowned cranes in Hokkaido every year. Groups of elementary school students are taken to many locations near the habitat of the crane, and they begin their count at the same time. In December 1987, 424 red-crowned cranes were spotted in Hokkaido.

Much has been done to protect the red-crowned

（財）日本野鳥の会

鶴居・伊藤

ダンチョウサンクチュアン

TANCHO SANCTUARY
WILD BIRD SOCIETY OF JAPAN

This sign marks the Tancho Sanctuary, which was established to help protect the red-crowned cranes of Hokkaido.

crane in Japan. Since 1952, some of the marshland in Hokkaido has been named a "special natural monument" by the Japanese government. And since 1967, the red-crowned crane has had the same protection. But even though the birds are protected, and the number of red-crowned cranes in Japan has increased, the dangers to their survi-

val have not ended. As many as 20 red-crowned cranes have been killed in one year when they flew into electric power lines. The lines are difficult for the birds to see when they are frightened and take off or change course suddenly.

Bird of Peace

The beauty of the red-crowned crane, and its scientific value as an indicator of the condition of wetlands, have focused international attention on the threats to its survival. Ornithologists and conservationists of many nations are working together to study and protect this remarkable bird. In one international project, the Soviet Union and China are working together to set up a park for the red-crowned crane. In many ways the red-crowned crane is providing opportunities for different countries to work together in peaceful cooperation.

Chapter 4

The Four Seasons of the Crane

Thick patches of snow are scattered over the marsh when the red-crowned cranes arrive there in early March. Some of the cranes return to last year's nesting area, while others find a new home in a quiet place away from other cranes and far from people.

Spring

In late March, a crane couple builds a nest on a hummock in the marsh. Here they crush down the grass with their feet and pull out tall reeds with their bills, and soon they have a large clear area for a nest. Now the two cranes work together, gathering grass, reeds, and twigs to make a nest more than three feet (about one meter) across, and

A red-crowned crane parent turns over an egg with its bill.

about 20 inches (51 centimeters) high. This construction work takes about a week.

The first egg appears early one morning in April or early May; two days later there are a pair of eggs in the nest. The eggs of the red-crowned crane are smooth, and they can be white, or tan and gray and covered with dark speckles. Crane eggs are almost three times larger than chicken eggs, and four times as heavy. Usually the red-crowned crane lays only two eggs, but if both eggs are destroyed, the crane may lay another pair.

The female crane usually keeps the eggs warm with her body at night, but during the day, the parents take turns sitting on the nest. About once an hour, the parent on the nest stands up and turns the eggs over with its bill so that the eggs are evenly warmed. Then the crane sits back down.

Crane parents are very alert when they are **incubating** eggs, and any animal that comes too close to the nesting area will be quickly chased away. Lowering its head to show its bright red crown, an angry parent will rush at an unwelcome visitor, and threaten it with its sharp claws and long bill.

After about four weeks, a tiny *shee-shee* sound can be heard from one of the eggs; it is almost time to hatch. Two or three days later, the chick makes a small hole in its shell, and after pecking at the opening for two days, the hole is large enough for the baby crane to wriggle out of its shell. The happy parents cannot hide their joy. Together they throw their heads into the air and trumpet a crane duet. Then the parents crush the empty shell with their feet and toss it out of the nest.

Although red-crowned cranes lay two eggs, usually only one of them will hatch. The other egg may be destroyed by a predator, or it may get cold in water from melting snow.

The baby crane is covered with light brown fluff, weighs about five ounces (150 grams), and stands about six inches (15 centimeters) tall. A few hours after it is born, the crane chick leaves its

nest. Staying close to its parents, the chick explores the area near the nest and gets its first taste of food. The little crane cannot walk very well, but its parents are not afraid if it falls into nearby water because the newborn crane is a good swimmer.

Summer

Baby cranes are born in late May or early June. The next three months are very busy for the parents because feeding a hungry crane chick is a lot of work. Crane babies eat and eat and eat. The baby birds can find some food by themselves soon after they are born, but not enough food for their needs. Their parents feed them insects, tiny fish, and other small animals. In just six weeks the baby red-crowned crane grows to more than three feet tall!

Summer is also the season when the adult cranes **molt**, or shed some of their feathers. While they are growing new wing feathers, the birds cannot fly well, and must be alert for predators that might attack the adults as well as the babies.

A red-crowned crane chick.

A baby crane stays close to its parents in the tall reeds and grasses of a marsh.

When the crane chick is about six weeks old, its light brown fluff begins to disappear, and the young crane grows real brown and white feathers. At this age, too, the young crane begins to flap its little wings. This exercise makes the wings strong for the bird's first flight when it is about three months old.

The first flight takes place in late August or early September when the young cranes follow their parents into the air. Soon the young fliers are taking off on their own. Red-crowned crane parents watch as a young bird circles above them, sometimes scolding it with a low-throated clucking sound to call the restless young one back to earth.

Autumn

By mid-September the young crane is almost as tall as its parents, but it still follows its mother with a *heep-peep, peep-peep.* Because its long trachea is not completely developed, the young bird cannot make the sounds of an adult. At this age it is mostly white or gray with a few scattered light brown feathers, and dark brown where the adult is black.

As the cool autumn days grow shorter in October and November, the red-crowned cranes in Hokkaido know that winter is on its way, and the shallow waters of the marsh will freeze. The crane family begins to move out of the marsh

This young crane has scattered light brown feathers.

and onto nearby farm fields in search of bits of corn or buckwheat that have been dropped in harvest.

Winter
In winter, snow covers the farm fields in Hokkaido, and many cranes would starve if some farmers did not put corn and buckwheat out for them

50

to eat. During December, January, and February, these farms become the gathering places for the red-crowned cranes in Japan.

Winter is a time for the cranes to relax. They have no nesting activities now, and their young can find their own food. On the snow-covered farm fields the red-crowned cranes spend much of their time eating. Now and then a bird makes a trumpet call, or begins the interesting motions of the crane dance. Sometimes fights break out on the field over food or space; the cranes do not like to be too close to each other.

When the sun starts to disappear behind the mountains of Hokkaido, the red-crowned cranes leave the farm fields in groups of one to three or four families, and fly to a nearby river where they **roost** for the night. The cranes sleep standing in the river in a spot where the water is not too swift, and where they are protected from the wind by high river banks. Here in the water they are safe from foxes and dogs. But the cranes sleep in the

After spending the night in a nearby river, a small group of red-crowned cranes flies back to the farm fields.

river for another reason, too; the moving water of the river is warmer than the winter air, and so the river provides warmth to the animals. To help keep warm, the cranes sleep with one leg pulled up under the body, which presses warm feathers even closer to their bodies. During the night the birds wake up from time to time and look around for danger. When they feel safe, they tuck their long bills under a wing and go back to sleep.

At dawn the cranes open their eyes and slowly become active. They stretch their broad wings, wade in the water, or walk along the river bank. The birds are not in a hurry to return to the farm fields for breakfast. It may be nine or ten o'clock before they fly to the fields in small groups to begin their daily winter feeding.

Back to the Marsh

In spring, the crane parents leave their young and return to the marsh in pairs. If a young red-crowned crane follows its parents to the nesting area, it is chased away like an enemy. When spring comes, the young cranes are on their own.

Back in the tall reeds of the marsh, an adult crane trumpets a loud call. Taking long, slow steps, and with its head held high, the graceful red-crowned crane seems to know it is a special animal.

Sources of Information about the Crane

Though the red-crowned crane and six other crane species around the world are endangered, one group has worked actively to protect them and ensure their survival. The International Crane Foundation (ICF) was founded in 1973 by two college students who set out to save the threatened crane species from extinction, as well as to learn more about these remarkable birds.

Since the ICF began, it has started useful programs in many areas of the world that were in danger of losing their crane populations. In China, Japan, Korea, and the Soviet Union, the ICF helped study and protect important breeding and wintering grounds for the red-crowned crane. In Tibet, the group located the last flock of the black-necked crane and helped preserve its habitat. These are only two examples of the many projects the ICF has organized.

In addition to these international efforts, the ICF raises many species in captivity at its headquarters in Baraboo, Wisconsin. The organization calls this part of the program a "species bank." Visitors to the large center can see crane chicks or watch videos about different crane species. There are also walking tours through the grounds where the cranes live, and lucky visitors may be able to see the famous crane dance.

For more information about the International Crane Foundation, its projects, and what you can do to help save the red-crowned crane and its relatives, write to the foundation headquarters.

International Crane Foundation
E-11376 Shady Lane Road
Baraboo, Wisconsin 53913

Glossary

Ainu (EYE-noo)—the native people of Hokkaido, Japan

camouflage (CAM-uh-flahj)—the coloring or appearance of an animal which helps it hide from predators or enemies

conservationist—one who studies and works for the preservation and protection of living things and their natural habitat

endangered—animals or plants that are so few in number they could become extinct

extinct (ehk-STINGKT)—no longer living anywhere on earth; many animal and plant species have become extinct

Gruidae (groo-EE-day)—the scientific name for the crane family

habitat—the area where an animal or plant naturally lives

hummock—a small, dry mound of earth

56

incubate (IHN-kyuh-bayt)—to keep eggs warm by sitting on them

kimono—a long silk gown that the Japanese wear on special occasions

mammals—warm-blooded animals with backbones and hair or fur; the females bear live young and produce milk to feed them

migrate—to move from one area to another for feeding or breeding

molt—to shed fur or feathers before they are replaced with new growth

omnivorous (ahm-NIV-ur-uhs)—to feed on both animals and plants

origami (ohr-ih-GAH-mee)—the Japanese craft of paper folding

ornithologist (ohr-nuh-THAHL-uh-jihst)—a scientist who studies birds

pollute—to make land, water, or air dirty or impure

predator (PREHD-uh-tuhr)—an animal that hunts other animals for food

prey—an animal that is hunted by another animal for food

roost—to settle down for rest or sleep

species—distinct kinds of animals or plants having common characteristics and a common name

sternum—breastbone; a bone in the chest which connects the ribs

trachea (TRAY-kee-uh)—the windpipe; the tube in the throat and chest that carries air to the lungs

wingspan—the distance across the wings from tip to tip when the wings are spread open

Index

About the Author

Edward Voeller is a lecturer at the Institute of Language and Culture Studies at Hokkaido University in Sapporo, Japan, and the editor of the *Sapporo Ambassador*. In preparation for this book, Mr. Voeller observed red-crowned cranes at close range in the marshes and farm fields of Hokkaido. He also photographed them during different seasons in their native habitat.

Voeller is a textbook writer and the author of numerous articles for Asian periodicals and the *Christian Science Monitor*. His educational background includes a B.A. in international relations, an M.A. in applied linguistics, and coursework toward a Ph.D. in journalism. Voeller also served in the Peace Corps in Thailand. He and his family now reside in Sapporo.